ACCESS CHINESE

汉语入门

Workbook │ 练习册 1

主 编：刘　骏 Jun Liu

编 者：魏慧萍 Wei Huiping

FOREIGN LANGUAGE TEACHING AND RESEARCH PRESS　BEIJING

McGraw-Hill Higher Education

ACCESS CHINESE WORKBOOK 1, FIRST EDITION

Co-Published by McGraw-Hill, an imprint of The McGraw-Hill Companies, Inc., 1221 Avenue of the Americas, New York, NY 10020 and Foreign Language Teaching and Research Press, No. 19 Xisanhuan Beilu, Beijing, China, 100089. Copyright © 2013 McGraw-Hill Companies, Inc. and Foreign Language Teaching and Research Press. Printed in China.

ISBN: 978-0-07-728802-0
MHID: 0-07-728802-5

McGraw-Hill:
Vice President, Products and Markets: Michael Ryan
Editorial Director: William R. Glass
Publisher: Katie Stevens
Senior Sponsoring Editor: Katherine K. Crouch
Senior Director of Development: Scott Tinetti
Development Editor: Jennifer Kirk
Editorial Coordinator: Erin Blaze
Executive Marketing Manager: Craig Gill
Faculty Development Manager: Jorge Arbujas

FLTRP:
Publisher: Cai Jianfeng
Editor in Chief: Xu Jianzhong
Project Planning: Man Xingyuan
Project Management: Ding Ning
Project Editor: Li Yang, Xie Danling
Editorial Supporting Team: Cai Ying, Liu Hongyan, Xu Yang, Yan Li, Yao Jun, Zhao Qing

Boston	Burr Ridge, IL	Dubuque, IA	Madison, WI	New York	San Francisco
St. Louis	Bangkok	Bogotá	Caracas	Kuala Lumpur	Lisbon
London	Madrid	Mexico City	Milan	Montreal	New Delhi
Santiago	Seoul	Singapore	Sydney	Taipei	Toronto

www.mhhe.com

www.fltrp.com
www.chineseplus.com

Contents 目录

Introduction to Pinyin

拼音介绍 …………………………………………………………………… 2

Introduction to Chinese Characters

汉字介绍 …………………………………………………………………… 9

Unit 1　Meeting Each Other

第一单元　见面寒暄 ……………………………………………………… 15

Unit 2　Gifts and Courtesy

第二单元　礼尚往来 ……………………………………………………… 27

Unit 3　Feel at Home Wherever You Are

第三单元　四海为家 ……………………………………………………… 40

Unit 4　In and Out of Class

第四单元　课内课外 ……………………………………………………… 51

Unit 5　Shopping and Bargaining

第五单元　讨价还价 ……………………………………………………… 62

Unit 6　Fine Food

第六单元　天下美食 ……………………………………………………… 75

Introduction to Pinyin

Pīn yīn jiè shào
拼 音 介 绍

Syllables

1 Combine initials and finals to create Chinese syllables, then listen and repeat each one.

zh + ōng → zhōng	q + īng →	m + ěi →
r + én →	g + uó →	b + ài →
h + àn →	c + án →	f + ǎ →
j + iā →	n + á →	d + à →

2 Write the initial and final of each syllable, then listen and repeat each one.

hé → h + é	zhuān →	huā →	dù →
yí →	zāng →	gè →	yāo →
zǒu →	qǐng →	biàn →	shuài →

Tones

3 Listen and repeat, then add the tone mark to each final or syllable.

ā o e i u ü

á o e i u ü

ǎ o e i u ü

à o e i u ü

wo ni ta ta
我 你 他 她

Wo e le.
我 饿 了。

Ni e ma?
你 饿 吗?

mama   baba   jiejie   didi
妈妈   爸爸   姐姐   弟弟

4 Listen carefully, then circle the syllable with the correct tone. 🎧

(1) (wèn) wěn   (3) guó guǒ   (5) mā mǎ   (7) yú yǔ

(2) yāo yào   (4) tāng táng   (6) suān suàn   (8) yuǎn yuàn

5 Listen and repeat, then add the tone mark to each syllable. Be sure to put the tone mark on the correct vowel. 🎧

(1) zhong guo hen da   (4) hua hong liu lü

(2) shan he mei li   (5) qian chui bai lian

(3) guang ming lei luo   (6) jian chi nu li

Initials

6 Listen to the recording and circle the correct initial. 🎧

(1) b (p) d   (3) z j zh   (5) s sh x   (7) h r k

(2) m n l   (4) c ch q   (6) g d k   (8) z c s

7 Listen carefully, then circle the syllable with the correct initial. 🎧

(1) (bā) pā   (5) mù nù   (9) jí qí   (13) zī zhī

(2) bō pō   (6) nǔ lǔ   (10) jǔ qǔ   (14) cí chí

(3) nà tà   (7) ní lí   (11) xī sī   (15) sì shì

(4) dú tú   (8) mó fó   (12) jù qù   (16) rì lì

8 Listen and repeat, paying careful attention to the pronunciation of the initials, finals and tones. 🎧

bēnpǎo	fāngbiàn	měilì	dàitì
nǔlì	kāiguān	kèkǔ	gàikuàng
huángguā	xuéxí	qīnqiè	xiūxi
jiāxiāng	jīqì	shānshuǐ	zǐxì
shēngqì	zìcí	qíshí	qìngzhù
wòshǒu	báiyún	xīnyuàn	hànyǔ

9 Listen carefully, then circle the correct final.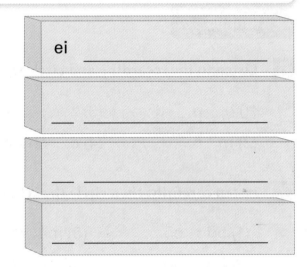

(1) a o ⓔ   (3) ai ao ei   (5) ie üe iu (iou)   (7) en eng ang

(2) u ü i   (4) an en in   (6) ia ie ian   (8) in ing iang

10 Read each syllable aloud, then categorize them based on their finals.

méi	yǒu	měi	hǎo	huā	kāi	zǒu	ài	kuài
lái	dōu	fēi	luó	wéi	duō	duì	wài	shuài
gěi	guà	zuì	zhāi	táo				

ai kāi _____

ei _____

___ _____

___ _____

___ _____

___ _____

___ _____

___ _____

11 Listen and repeat.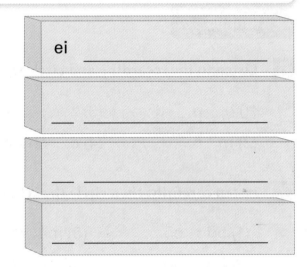

ai   ei   ao   ou   ua   uo   uai   ui (uei)

tài   fēi   bǎo   tóu   huà   duó   wài   duì   shuǐ

12 Read each syllable aloud, then categorize them based on their finals.

juǎn	quān	yào	xuán	yuè	jié	jiā
yuǎn	jiào	jiǔ	xiù	jiào	xué	yá
yě	xiào	jiù	qiú	yǒu		

ia yá jiā _____

ie _____

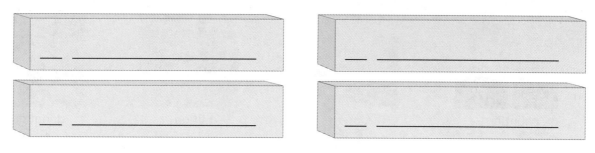

13 **Listen and repeat.** 🎧

ia   ie   iao   iu (iou)   üe   üan

qià   xiě   jiāo   jiǔ   yuè   jiào   juàn   qiáo   yuǎn

14 **Listen carefully, then circle the syllable with the correct final.** 🎧

(1) (tán) táng   (5) yǔn yǒng   (9) yōu yuē   (13) wàn yuàn

(2) shēn shēng   (6) wēn wēng   (10) yào yuè   (14) zhēn zhēng

(3) jǐn jǐng   (7) yǐn yǐng   (11) táo tiáo   (15) téng tóng

(4) wàn wàng   (8) zhèn zhèng   (12) tōu tuō   (16) yú yóu

Words and Sentences

15 **Try to read the following words by yourself first, and then listen and repeat each one after the recording.** 🎧

píngguǒ
苹果
apple

kāfēi
咖啡
coffee

shǒujī
手机
cell phone

diànnǎo
电脑
computer

lánqiú
篮球
basketball

yīfu
衣服
clothes

dàhǎi
大海
sea

shǒu
手
hand

chūntiān
春天
spring

xiàtiān
夏天
summer

qiūtiān
秋天
fall

dōngtiān
冬天
winter

tàiyáng
太阳
sun

dìqiú
地球
earth

yuèliang
月亮
moon

yǎn
眼
eye

16 Listen carefully and decide whether the tone marks are written correctly. If not, rewrite the words with the correct tone marks. 🎧

(1) yīshēng _____   (3) yìgè _____   (5) bútīng _____   (7) bùxiě _____

(2) yìnián _____   (4) yìqǐ _____   (6) bùxíng _____   (8) bùqù _____

17 Listen and repeat, then fill in the blanks with the correct initials, finals and tone marks. 🎧

(1) A: Nǐ hǎo! Wǒ ___ì Lǐ Lì. ___ǒ shì Zhōngguór___.

   B: Nǐ hǎo! Wǒ shì Bǐ'ěr. Wǒ shì M___guórén.

(2) A: Wǒ xǐh___ huàhuàr. Nǐ n___?

   B: Wǒ xǐhuan ___àn diànyǐng. ___uìjìn yǒu y___ bù diànyǐng hěn ___ǎokàn.

(3) A: Wǒ yǒudiǎnr ___ le. Nǐ è ma?

   B: Wǒ b___ è. Wǒ yǒudiǎn___ kě.

Listen to the recording and read silently. Listen again and repeat the tongue twisters.

18

汤烫塔

老唐端蛋汤，
踏凳登宝塔。
只因凳太滑，
汤洒汤烫塔。

Tāng tàng tǎ

Lǎo Táng duān dàntāng,
tà dèng dēng bǎotǎ.
Zhǐ yīn dèng tài huá,
tāng sǎ tāng tàng tǎ.

19

四和十，十和四，
十四和四十，四十和十四。
谁说四十是"细席"，
他的舌头没用力；
谁说十四是"实事"，
他的舌头没伸直。
认真学，常练习，
十四、四十、四十四。

Sì hé shí, shí hé sì,
shísì hé sìshí, sìshí hé shísì.
Shéi shuō sìshí shì "xìxí",
tā de shétou méi yònglì;
Shéi shuō shísì shì "shíshì",
tā de shétou méi shēn zhí.
Rènzhēn xué, cháng liànxí,
shísì, sìshí, sìshísì.

20

哥哥弟弟坡前坐。
坡上卧着一只鹅。
坡下流着一条河。
哥哥说："宽宽的河。"
弟弟说："白白的鹅。"
鹅要过河，河要渡鹅。
不知是鹅过河，
还是河渡鹅。

Gēge dìdi pō qián zuò.
Pō shang wòzhe yì zhī é.
Pō xià liúzhe yì tiáo hé.
Gēge shuō: "Kuānkuān de hé."
Dìdi shuō: "Báibái de é."
É yào guò hé, hé yào dù é.
Bùzhī shì é guò hé,
háishi hé dù é.

Congratulations!

Now that you have completed the practice activities for *Introduction to Pinyin*, please answer the following questions to see how much you know about Pinyin.

How many tones can you find in Chinese syllables?

_____

What's the zero-initial syllable?

_____

Can you write down the real final which appears in *jú*, *qǔ*, *xū*?

_____

Read the sentence below:

Wǒ hěn xǐhuan shuō Hànyǔ.

GREAT!

Introduction to Chinese Characters

Hàn zì jiè shào

汉字介绍

Images of Chinese Characters

1 Match the modern Chinese characters with the corresponding ancient characters.

日　口　山　水　人　目　羊　月　车

2 Classify the characters into their corresponding structure types.

人　作　手　奋　运　国　森
告　围　辨　旧　掰　旭　磊

Single-element: 木 _____

Upper-lower: 字 _____

Total-enclosed: 因 _____

Left-middle-right: 树 _____

Left-right: 你 _____

Semi-enclosed: 这 _____

Structure like 品: 众 _____

3 Match each simple character with its corresponding radical form, then match the radical with the proper compound character.

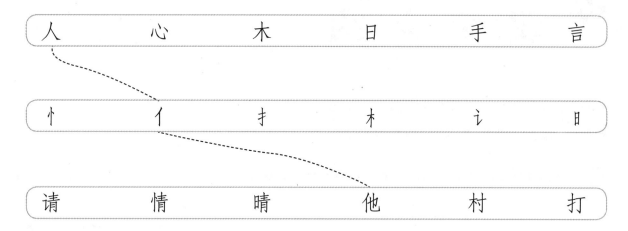

4 Write the number and letter that correspond to each component of the following characters.

信 ①a　迫＿＿＿　情＿＿＿　沐＿＿＿　捂＿＿＿　泊＿＿＿

河＿＿＿　语＿＿＿　倩＿＿＿　拍＿＿＿　打＿＿＿　清＿＿＿

悟＿＿＿　怕＿＿＿　休＿＿＿　请＿＿＿　江＿＿＿　远＿＿＿

①亻　②氵　③讠　④忄　⑤扌　⑥辶

a. 言　b. 木　c. 青　d. 白　e. 吾　f. 可　g. 工　h. 丁　i. 元

Chinese Characters and Meanings

5 Match each character with its general meaning.

森	to taste	说	to be happy
品	forest	悦	to take off
众	many people	脱	to speak
他	ground	清	please
她	he	请	feeling
地	she	情	the water is clear

6 Explain the general meaning of each group of characters based on the radical.

清	江	河	海	泪	油	about water or liquid
眼	晴	盯	瞪	瞄	睁	_____
草	花	苗	茶	艾	芋	_____
追	近	远	速	达	迎	_____
唱	吟	叫	喊	味	问	_____
家	安	宁	宝	守	宅	_____

Strokes and Stroke Order

---

7 Write the basic strokes.

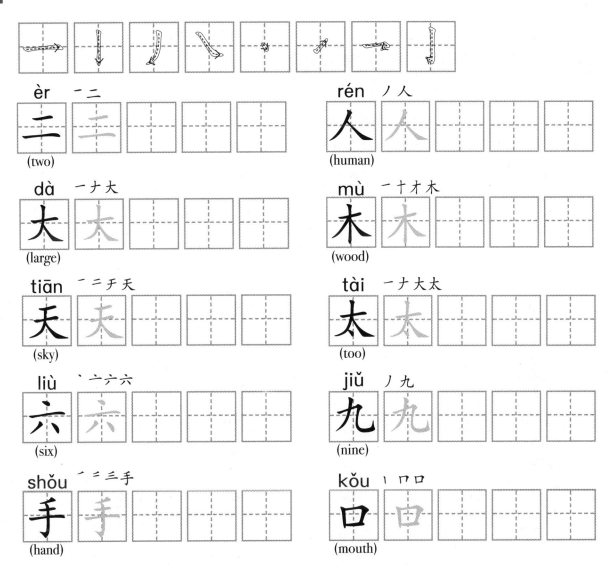

èr 一 二
(two)

rén ノ 人
(human)

dà 一 ナ 大
(large)

mù 一 十 才 木
(wood)

tiān 一 二 チ 天
(sky)

tài 一 ナ 大 太
(too)

liù 丶 一 六 六
(six)

jiǔ ノ 九
(nine)

shǒu 一 二 三 手
(hand)

kǒu 丨 冂 口
(mouth)

8 Say the general principles aloud while writing the characters with the correct stroke order.

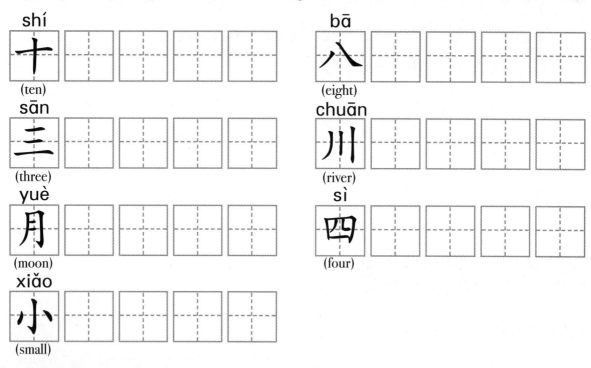

shí
十
(ten)

bā
八
(eight)

sān
三
(three)

chuān
川
(river)

yuè
月
(moon)

sì
四
(four)

xiǎo
小
(small)

Reading and Writing the Characters

9 Read the following characters aloud, then write each character, paying special attention to the differences between each pair.

zuǒ   yòu
左 (left)   —   右 (right)

shǒu   máo
手 (hand)   —   毛 (wool)

yǒu   fǎn
友 (friend)   —   反 (contrary)

yún   qù
云 (cloud)   —   去 (to go)

wèi   mò
未 (not yet)   —   末 (end)

yùn   yuǎn
运 (to move)   —   远 (far)

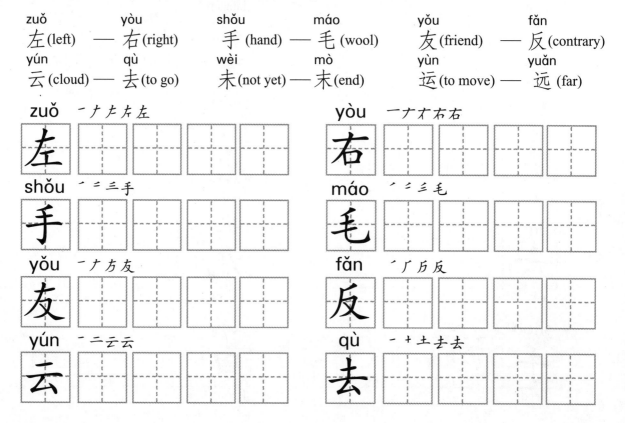

zuǒ 一 ナ た ち 左
左

yòu 一 ナ ナ 右 右
右

shǒu ノ 二 三 手
手

máo ノ 二 三 毛
毛

yǒu 一 ナ 方 友
友

fǎn ノ 厂 戶 反
反

yún 一 二 云 云
云

qù 一 十 土 去 去
去

wèi	一 二 十 才 未					mò	一 二 十 才 末				
未						末					
yùn	一 二 云 云 运 运 运					yuǎn	一 二 テ 元 元 远 远				
运						远					

10 Listen and read. Then practice writing the characters.

(1) A： Nǐ hǎo!
　　　你好！

　　B： Nǐ hǎo!
　　　你好！

(2) A： Jīntiān zhōu jǐ?
　　　今天 周 几？

　　B： Jīntiān Zhōuwǔ.
　　　今天 周五。

(3) A： Wǒ shì Zhōngguórén.
　　　我 是 中国人。

　　B： Wǒ shì Měiguórén.
　　　我 是 美国人。

(1) A: Hello!
　　B: Hello!
(2) A: What day is today?
　　B: Today is Friday.
(3) A: I am Chinese.
　　B: I am American.

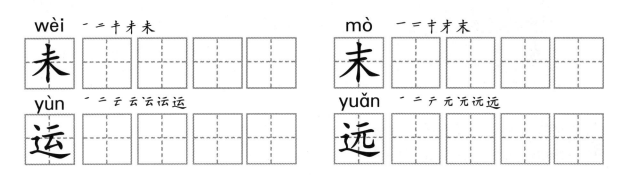

nǐ	ノ イ イ' 亻' 你 你 你					hǎo	乚 刀 女 女' 奵 好				
你						好					
jīn	ノ 人 仐 今					tiān	一 二 于 天				
今						天					
zhōu	) 刀 刀 尸 月 用 周 周					wǔ	一 丁 五 五				
周						五					
sān	一 二 三					wǒ	一 二 千 才 我 我 我				
三						我					
shì	丨 口 日 旦 早 异 是 是					zhōng	丨 口 口 中				
是						中					
měi	丶 丷 丷 丷 丷 羊 美 美 美					guó	丨 冂 冂 冃 冃 国 国 国				
美						国					

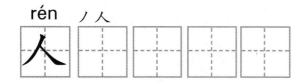

rén ノ人

Calligraphy Appreciation

11 Try to distinguish the three common script types of modern Chinese characters presented below.

níngjìng zhìyuǎn
宁静 致远   Inner peace reaches afar.

Congratulations!

Now that you have completed the practice activities for *Introduction to Chinese Characters*, please answer the following questions to see how much you know about Chinese characters.

What are the main features of Chinese characters?

_____

How do radicals help determine the meanings of characters?

_____

Is stroke order important in writing characters? Why or why not?

_____

Write some of the characters that you remember from *Introduction to Chinese Characters*.

GREAT!

Unit 1   Meeting Each Other

Dì-yī dānyuán   Jiàn miàn hán xuān

第一单元   见 面 寒 暄

Pronunciation Practice

1 Listen carefully and mark the correct tones for the characters, following the example.

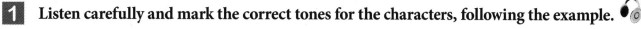

他	您	我	你	汉	语	名	字

没	有	请	问	电	话	号	码

高	兴	见	到	是	姓	很	也

2 Listen and read, then circle the characters pronounced with the neutral tone.

漂亮   什么   多少   哪里哪里

你的   他们   吃了   好吗

3 Read the phrases and circle the characters pronounced with the 3rd tone. Then underline the characters with a change in the 3rd tone.

hěn gāoxìng
很 高兴

wǒ hěn hǎo
我 很 好

nǐ de Hànyǔ hěn hǎo
你 的 汉语 很 好

nǐ jiào shénme
你 叫 什么

wǒ yě hěn hǎo
我 也 很 好

nǎli nǎli
哪里哪里

4 Write the Pinyin for each character, and then classify the syllables according to their initials.

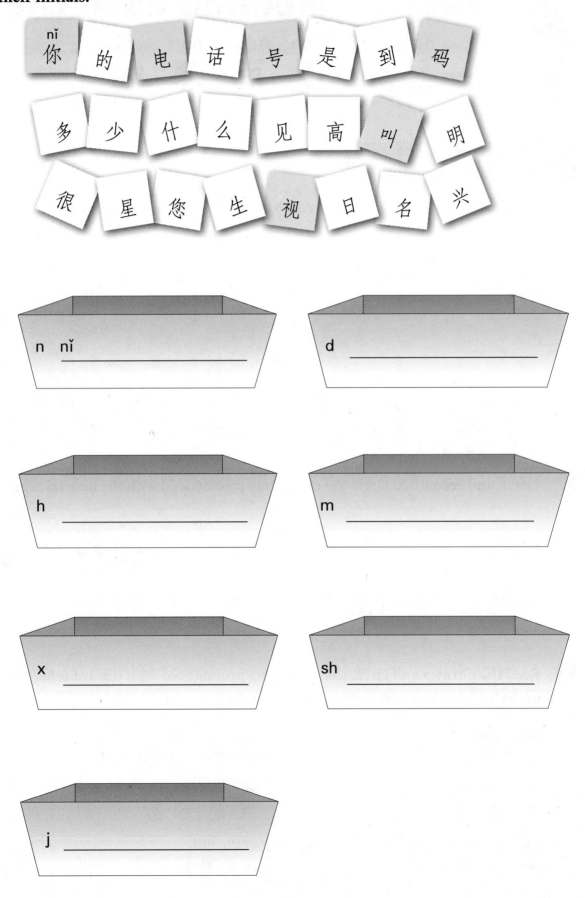

你 的 电 话 号 是 到 码

多 少 什 么 见 高 叫 明

很 星 您 生 视 日 名 兴

n nǐ _____

d _____

h _____

m _____

x _____

sh _____

j _____

5 Write the Pinyin for each character based on the recording, and then classify the syllables according to their tones.

tā 她	wo 我
yu 语	ta 他
piao 漂	hao 好
na 哪	han 汉
wen 问	ai 爱
xing 姓	mei 美
liang 亮	ke 可
qing 请	ma 吗
li 里	shuai 帅
shi 市	cheng 城

一声 ˉ   tā _____

二声 ´ _____

三声 ˇ _____

四声 ` _____

轻声 _____

6 Listen carefully to the recording, then match the Chinese characters with the correct Pinyin.

请问 ---->	qǐngwèn
名字	jiào
叫	shì
姓	diànhuà
电话	hàomǎ
是	míngzi
号码	xìng
什么	gāoxìng
高兴	shénme

好 ---->	hǎo
早上	nǐ
你	piàoliang
她	zǎoshang
漂亮	shuài
帅	tā
见到	hěn
很	duōshao
多少	jiàndào

7 Choose the correct Pinyin for each sentence.

①A: 你好!
○B: 您好!

○A: 早上好!
○B: 早上好!

○A: 见到你很高兴。
○B: 我也很高兴。

○A: 你叫什么名字?
○B: 我叫李丽。

○A: 你的电话号码是多少?
○B: 5079608。

○她很漂亮。他很帅。

①Nǐ hǎo!

②Nǐ jiào shénme míngzi?

③Nín hǎo!

④Wǒ yě hěn gāoxìng.

⑤Jiàndào nǐ hěn gāoxìng.

⑥Wǒ jiào Lǐ Lì.

⑦Zǎoshang hǎo!

⑧Nǐ de diànhuà hàomǎ shì duōshao?

⑨Tā hěn piàoliang. Tā hěn shuài.

⑩Wǔ líng qī jiǔ liù líng bā.

Vocabulary Practice

8 Match the Chinese words to their correct English definitions.

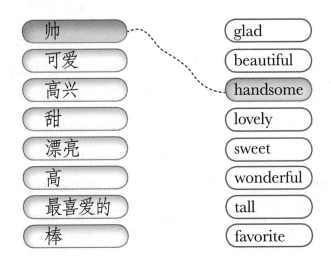

帅	———	glad
可爱		beautiful
高兴		handsome
甜		lovely
漂亮		sweet
高		wonderful
最喜爱的		tall
棒		favorite

9 Match the appropriate characters to create words.

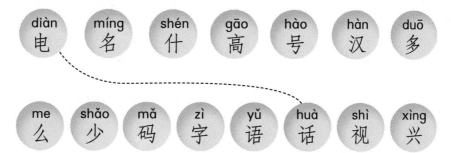

diàn 电 míng 名 shén 什 gāo 高 hào 号 hàn 汉 duō 多

me 么 shǎo 少 mǎ 码 zi 字 yǔ 语 huà 话 shì 视 xìng 兴

10 Listen to the recording and match the words with the appropriate pictures.

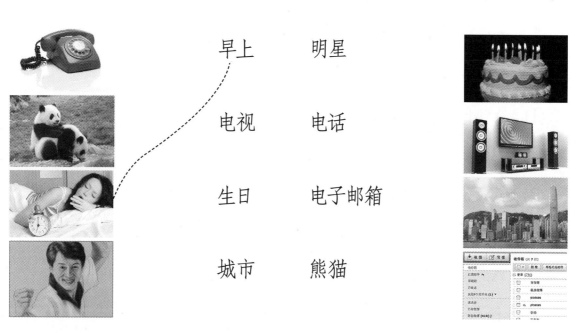

早上　　明星

电视　　电话

生日　　电子邮箱

城市　　熊猫

Grammar Practice

11 Complete the sentences.

(1) 你好! 你＿＿＿＿＿＿什么名字?

　　a. 是　　　　　　b. 姓　　　　　　c. 叫

(2) 见到你很＿＿＿＿＿＿。

　　a. 漂亮　　　　　b. 甜　　　　　　c. 高兴

(3) 你＿＿＿＿＿＿比尔吗?

　　a. 很　　　　　　b. 他　　　　　　c. 是

(4) 你很漂亮，她_____很漂亮。

    a.也   b.是   c.不

(5) A：你的汉语很好。   B：_____。

    a.什么什么   b.很好   c.哪里哪里

12 **Complete the dialogues with the given words.**

> 是   吗

eg. A：他<u>是</u>李明<u>吗</u>?

    B：他<u>是</u>李明。

(1) A：你_____比尔_____?

     B：我_____比尔。

(2) A：她_____李丽_____?

     B：她_____李丽。

(3) A：你的电话号码_____50662889_____?

     B：_____。

(4) A：李丽_____中国人_____?

     B：李丽_____中国人。

13 **Complete the passage with the given words.**

> 是   叫   很   也   的

    李丽_____中国人，她_____可爱。Bill_____美国人，他_____汉语名字_____比尔，他_____帅。Courtney_____是美国人，她的汉语_____好。比尔见到李丽_____高兴。Courtney见到比尔_____很高兴。

14 Create some Chinese names with the given information.

> **Surnames:**
>
> | Zhāng | Wáng | Lǐ | Zhào | Liú | Chén |
> |---|---|---|---|---|---|
> | 张 | 王 | 李 | 赵 | 刘 | 陈 |
>
> **Given names:**
>
> | Xiǎolì | Qiáng | Jūn | Fāngfāng | Zǐhán | Dàwěi | Xīnyí |
> |---|---|---|---|---|---|---|
> | 小丽 | 强 | 军 | 芳芳 | 子涵 | 大伟 | 心怡 |

> *For your reference:*
>
> 丽: beautiful 强: strong 军: army 芳: fragrance
>
> 涵: to contain 伟: great 怡: happy

For girls	For boys

15 Write complete sentences to describe the people in the pictures.

高   可爱   漂亮   帅   很

Lín Miàokě
林 妙可＿＿＿

Yáo Míng
姚 明＿＿＿

Tāmen
她们＿＿＿

Láng Lǎng
郎 朗＿＿＿

＿＿＿＿＿。   ＿＿＿＿＿。   ＿＿＿＿＿。   ＿＿＿＿＿。

16 **Read the numbers in Chinese.**

Bus schedule

License plate number

Passport number

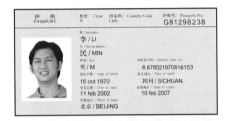

Price tag

Calendar

Cell phone contact list

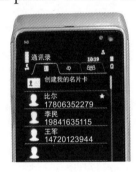

Writing Chinese Characters

17 **Write the sentences in Chinese, then read each one aloud.**

You want to make sure whether the girl is Li Li or not. You would ask:

_____

You want to know whether Bill is tall or not. You would ask:

_____

You want to tell Li Li she is beautiful. You would say:

_____

You feel Bill is very good at Chinese. You would say:

_____

18 **Practice writing the following Chinese characters.**

nǐ ノ イ 亻 伒 佫 你 你

你

wǒ ′ 二 手 手 我 我 我

我

míng ′ ク タ タ 名 名

名

zì ′ 丶 宀 宀 字 字

字

diàn 丨 冂 冃 日 电

电

huà 丶 讠 讠 讠 讠 话 话 话

话

hào 丨 冂 口 旦 号

号

mǎ 一 ノ イ 石 石 码 码 码

码

hàn 丶 丶 氵 沪 汉

汉

yǔ 丶 讠 讠 讠 讠 语 语 语

语

xìng 乚 女 女 女 妁 奵 姅 姓

姓

jiào 丨 冂 口 叫 叫

叫

jiàn 丨 冂 贝 见

见

dào 一 乙 互 丢 至 至 到 到

到

gāo 丶 亠 古 古 古 高 高 高 高

高

xìng 丶 丶 丷 兴 兴 兴

兴

shì 丨 冂 日 日 旦 早 昌 是 是

是

yǒu 一 ナ 才 有 有 有

有

piào 丶 丶 氵 沪 沪 沪 漂 漂 漂 漂 漂 漂

漂

liàng 丶 亠 亠 古 古 高 亭 亮

亮

hǎo 乚 女 女 妅 好 好

好

yě 丁 也 也

也

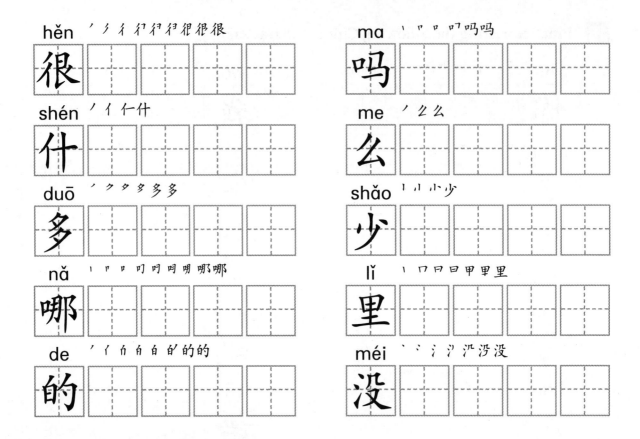

hěn 很	ノ ク 彳 彳 彳 彳 彳 很 很 很				

ma 吗	l 口 口 叮 吗 吗				

shén 什	ノ イ 仁 什				

me 么	ノ 乀 么				

duō 多	ノ ク タ タ 多 多				

shǎo 少	l 小 小 少				

nǎ 哪	l 口 口 叮 叨 叨 咿 哪 哪				

lǐ 里	l 口 日 日 甲 甲 里				

de 的	ノ イ 白 白 白 白 的 的				

méi 没	` 丶 氵 沕 沒 没				

Interpersonal Communication

19 Complete the conversation with your new Chinese friend Li Ming (李明) by filling in the blanks. Don't forget to write your Chinese name before each of your lines of the dialogue!

李明：　你好！

　　　：　_____！

李明：　请问，你叫什么名字？

　　　：　_____？

李明：　见到你很高兴。

　　　：　_____。

李明：　你的汉语很好。

　　　：　_____。

李明：　你的电话号码是多少？

　　　：　_____？

李明：　好，常联系。

　　　：　_____。

> **Tip**
>
> Cháng　liánxì.
> 常　　联系。
> Hope to keep in touch
> with you.

20 **Interview and discover.**

(1) Interview three classmates in your Chinese class. Ask their Chinese names and find out what they means.

	English Name	Chinese Name	The Meaning of Chinese Name
1			
2			
3			

(2) Give compliments to three classmates and record their answers.

	Name	Compliment	The Answer
1		你很棒!	
2		你很漂亮!	
3		你很可爱!	

(3) Which do you think is the best way to respond to a compliment from your Chinese friends? Why?

a. 哪里哪里。

b. 谢谢。

c. 我很高兴。

d. 没有没有。

Congratulations!

Now that you have completed the practice activities for Unit 1, please complete the following self-assessment to see how much you know.

Listen to the recording and repeat the sentences you hear. Then read the responses and choose the correct reply for each question or statement. 🎧

1. A: 你好！我是李丽。见到你很高兴。

   B: _____

2. A: 请问，你姓什么？

   B: _____

3. A: 你的汉语很好。

   B: _____

4. A: 你的电话号码是多少？

   B: _____

5. A: 他叫什么名字？

   B: _____

6. A: 您吃了吗?

   B: _____

哪里哪里。

我姓李。

吃了。

你好！我叫比尔。见到你我也很高兴。

2786926。

他叫李明。

你很棒！

Unit 2　Gifts and Courtesy

Dì-èr dānyuán　　Lǐ　shàng　wǎng　lái

第二单元　礼　尚　往　来

1　Listen carefully and mark the tone on each syllable. Then circle the characters that are pronounced with neutral tone. 🎧

妈妈	阿姨	朋友	谢谢	请客	你们	多大

好的	手机	心意	认识	女朋友	希望	喜欢

2　Read the sentences aloud and circle the syllables and characters pronounced with the initials *zh*, *ch*, *sh*.

(1)　A:　Zhè shì shénme?
　　　这 是 什么 ？

　　　B:　Zhè shì Zhōngguó dìtú, sòng gěi nǐ.
　　　这 是 中国 地图，送 给 你。

(2)　A:　Nǐ xǐhuan kàn shū ma?
　　　你 喜欢 看 书 吗？

　　　B:　Shìde, wǒ xǐhuan kàn shū.
　　　是的，我 喜欢 看 书。

(3)　A:　Zhè shì Zhōngguó chá, sòng gěi nǐ, qǐng shōuxià!
　　　这 是 中国 茶，送 给 你，请 收下！

　　　B:　Nǐ zhēn hǎo. Xièxie nǐ!
　　　你 真 好。谢谢 你！

3 Listen carefully and write the Pinyin for each character. Then classify the syllables according to their initials.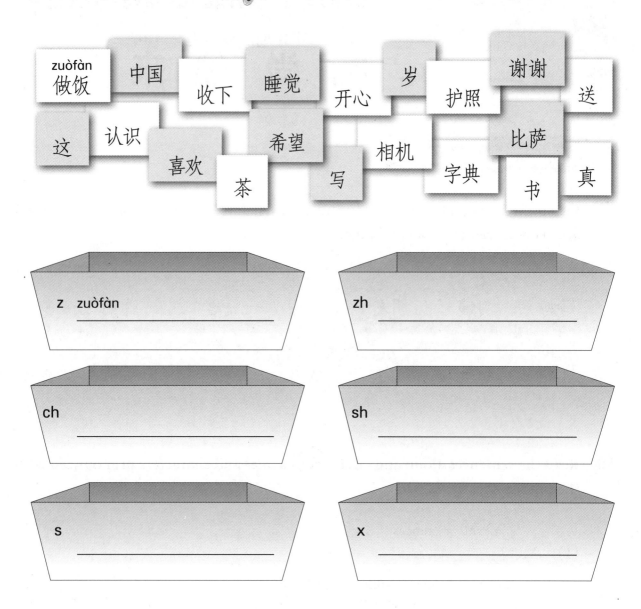

zuòfàn
做饭 中国 收下 睡觉 开心 岁 护照 谢谢 送
这 认识 希望 相机 比萨 字典 书 真
喜欢 茶 写

z   zuòfàn
_____

zh
_____

ch
_____

sh
_____

s
_____

x
_____

4 Say the names of the following objects in Chinese, and then write the Pinyin of each word.

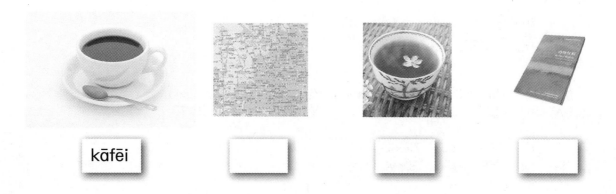

kāfēi

5 Listen carefully to the recording, then match the Chinese characters with the correct Pinyin.

地图 ------> dìtú

中国　　xīwàng

今天　　péngyou

朋友　　jīntiān

请客　　Zhōngguó

希望　　sòng gěi

送给　　qǐngkè

喝茶 ------> hē chá

比萨　　qiánbāo

护照　　shū

书　　　bǐsà

钱包　　xièxie

手机　　hùzhào

谢谢　　shǒujī

Vocabulary Practice

6 Listen to the recording, then rearrange the sentences in the correct order.

Zhēnnī,　nǐ jīntiān zhēn piàoliang!
① 珍妮，你今天 真 漂亮！

Zhè shì shénme?
○ 这 是 什么？

Xièxie!　Nǐ jīntiān yě hěn piàoliang!
○ 谢谢！你今天 也很 漂亮！

Zhè shì sòng gěi nǐ de lǐwù —— Zhōngguó chá.
○ 这 是 送 给你的礼物—— 中国 茶。

Wǒ xǐhuan hē chá.　Xièxie nǐ!
○ 我 喜欢 喝茶。谢谢 你！

7 Match each picture to the appropriate adjective.

niánqīng	kāixīn	měi	yōumò	gāo	bàng
年轻	开心	美	幽默	高	棒

8 Describe the people and objects in the pictures using 真+adjective.

漂亮　美　高　高兴　棒　幽默

花真美。_____

他们_____

她_____

他_____

他_____

他_____

9 **Match the appropriate characters to create words.**

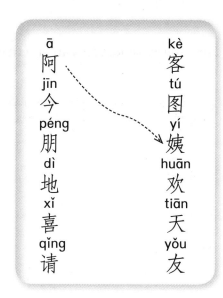

ā 阿	kè 客
jīn 今	tú 图
péng 朋	yí 姨
dì 地	huān 欢
xǐ 喜	tiān 天
qǐng 请	yǒu 友

xī 希	yì 意
qián 钱	jiǎng 奖
xīn 心	wàng 望
rèn 认	xià 下
guò 过	bāo 包
shōu 收	shí 识

10 **Complete the questions with 这 or 这些. Then answer the questions according to the pictures.**

(1) A: ＿＿＿是什么?

B: ＿＿＿＿＿＿。

(2) A: ＿＿＿是什么?

B: ＿＿＿＿＿＿。

(3) A: ＿＿＿是什么?

B: ＿＿＿＿＿＿。

(4) A: ＿＿＿是什么?

B: ＿＿＿＿＿＿。

(5) A: ＿＿＿是什么?

B: ＿＿＿＿＿＿。

11 Create at least six sentences using the given words. How many sentences can you make?

zhè	shì	wǒ	de	shū	hùzhào	Lǐ Lì	piàoliang	zhēn	gāo	Yáo Míng
这	是	我	的	书	护照	李丽	漂亮	真	高	姚明

wǒ	nǐ	xǐhuan	hē	kāfēi	yě	duō dà	jīnnián
我	你	喜欢	喝	咖啡	也	多大	今年

eg.
Zhè shì wǒ de shū.
这 是 我 的 书。

(1) _____   (4) _____

(2) _____   (5) _____

(3) _____   (6) _____

12 Complete the sentences using 也 or 都. Then follow the model to describe the people pictured below.

eg. 妈妈很漂亮, 阿姨_也_很漂亮。她们_都_很漂亮。

比尔是我的朋友, 李丽____是我的朋友。他们____是我的朋友。

我喜欢写汉字, 她____喜欢写汉字。我们____喜欢写汉字。

Yáo Míng
姚 明

Kēbǐ
科比

Zhāng Zǐyí

章 子怡

Xú Jìnglěi

徐 静蕾

Àobāmǎ

奥巴马

Bùshí

布什

13 **Create questions using** 什么 **according to the sentences given.**

Zhè shì dìtú.
(1) 这 是 地图。　　　　Question: _____?

Nà shì hùzhào.
(2) 那 是 护照。　　　　Question: _____?

Wǒ hē kělè.
(3) 我 喝 可乐。　　　　Question: _____?

Tā hē kāfēi.
(4) 他 喝 咖啡。　　　　Question: _____?

Wǒmen xǐhuan Hànyǔ.
(5) 我们 喜欢 汉语。　　　Question: _____?

Tā xǐhuan Zhōngguó chá.
(6) 她 喜欢 中国 茶。　　　Question: _____?

14 Complete the dialogues with the given words.

送给　　什么　　也　　呢　　谢谢

A: 这是_____你的礼物。

B: 是_____?

A: 是汉语字典。

B: _____你! 我很喜欢汉语, 你_____?

A: 我_____喜欢汉语。

吗　　吧　　呢

A: 你喜欢喝可乐_____?

B: 不喜欢, 你_____?

A: 我也是。

B: 我们喝茶_____。

Practical Training — Introduce Someone Using 这是

15 Help Wang Jun introduce his friends using 这是.

王大民: 珍妮, 这是我妈妈。

Lǐ　Xiǎohóng　　　Wáng　Jūn　　　Zhāng　Fāngfāng
李　小红　　　王　军　　　张　芳芳

(1)　Wang Jun wants to introduce Li Xiaohong to Zhang Fangfang:

_____.

(2)　Wang Jun wants to introduce Zhang Fangfang to Li Xiaohong:

_____.

Writing Chinese Characters

16 **Write the sentences in Chinese, then read each one aloud.**

You want to give gifts to your friend. You would say:

_____

In China, you want to know someone's age. You would ask:

_____

You got some gifts from your friend. You would say:

_____

You want to know whether your friend likes to drink tea or not. You would ask:

_____

17 **Practice writing the following Chinese characters.**

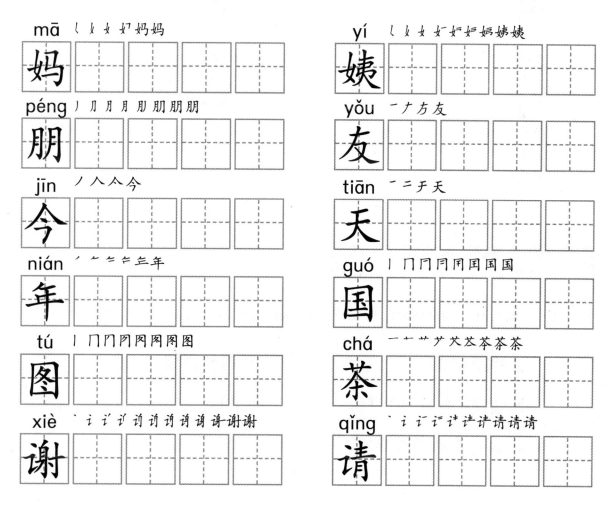

mā　ㄥ ㄥ 女 女 妈 妈
妈

yí　ㄥ ㄥ 女 女 妒 妒 姨 姨 姨
姨

péng　丿 刀 月 月 刖 朋 朋 朋
朋

yǒu　一 ナ 方 友
友

jīn　丿 人 仒 今
今

tiān　一 二 于 天
天

nián　丿 仁 仁 仨 年
年

guó　丨 冂 冂 同 用 国 国 国
国

tú　丨 冂 冂 冈 図 図 图
图

chá　一 十 艹 艹 芥 苤 苶 茶 茶
茶

xiè　丶 讠 讠 讠 访 询 询 询 谢 谢
谢

qǐng　丶 讠 讠 讠 诗 请 请 请 请
请

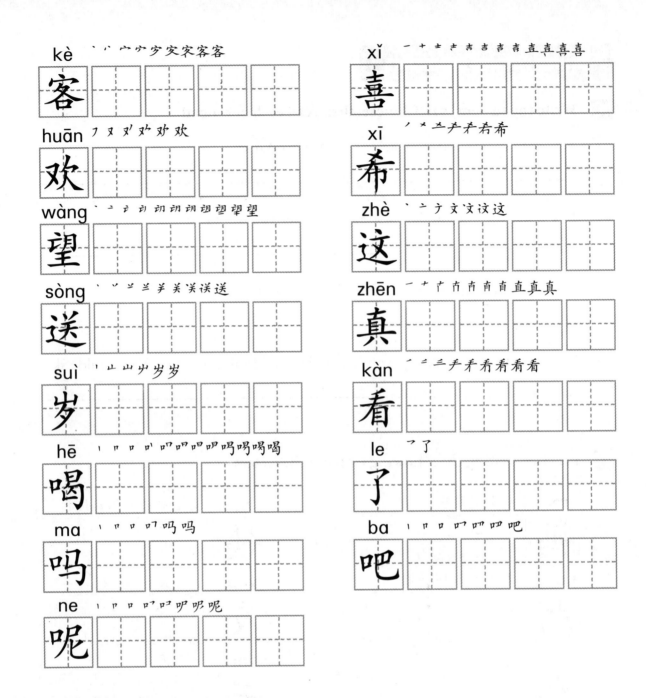

kè	客	`、` `宀` `宀` `灾` `灾` `客` `客` `客`
huān	欢	`フ` `ヌ` `ヌ'` `ヌ欠` `欢` `欢`
wàng	望	`、` `亠` `亅` `钉` `钊` `钥` `钥` `望` `望` `望`
sòng	送	`、` `丷` `ソ` `兰` `关` `关` `送` `送` `送`
suì	岁	`l` `山` `山` `岁` `岁` `岁`
hē	喝	`l` `ll` `lll` `l口` `l阝` `l阝` `吗` `喝` `喝` `喝` `喝`
ma	吗	`l` `ll` `lll` `l口` `吗` `吗`
ne	呢	`l` `ll` `lll` `l口` `l尸` `l尺` `l呢` `呢`

xǐ	喜	`一` `十` `土` `丰` `吉` `吉` `吉` `吉` `壹` `喜` `喜` `喜`
xī	希	`丿` `ㄨ` `兰` `产` `齐` `希` `希`
zhè	这	`、` `亠` `文` `文` `讠` `这` `这`
zhēn	真	`一` `十` `广` `市` `市` `肖` `肖` `直` `真` `真`
kàn	看	`、` `二` `三` `手` `手` `看` `看` `看` `看`
le	了	`フ` `了`
ba	吧	`l` `ll` `lll` `l口` `l吧` `l吧` `吧`

Interpersonal Communication

18 **Complete the conversations with the correct responses from the box.**

a. 哪里哪里。

b. 谢谢！你太客气了！

c. 我也喜欢喝咖啡。

d. 阿姨您好！

e. 20岁。

(1) A: 珍妮，这是我妈妈。

B: _____

(2) A: 阿姨，您真漂亮！

B: _____

(3) A: 你今年多大了？

B: _____

(4) A: 我喜欢喝咖啡，你呢？

B: _____

(5) A: 这是送给你的礼物。

B: _____

19 **Bill wants to give a gift to Li Li. Give him some suggestions on how to have the dialogue with Li Li in Chinese.**

比尔：李丽，这是_____。

李丽：送给我的礼物？是什么？

比尔：是_____，

希望_____。

李丽：我很喜欢看书。谢谢你！

比尔：_____。我也谢谢你送给我中国地图。这是礼尚往来！

20 **Interview and discover.**

(1) Interview three classmates in your Chinese class who come from different cultural backgrounds. Ask them to tell you their ages and record their answers and summarize your findings.

The question: 请问，你今年多大了？
The answer:

	姓名	国籍 (nationality)	回答 (answer)
1			
2			
3			
4			
5			

How did your friends respond to your questions? Get a conclusion:

_____

_____

_____

(2) Interview three friends, asking what they like to do.

The question: 你喜欢……吗？
Some useful words:

hē chá　　kàn shū　　gòuwù　　zuò fàn　　dǎ diànwán　　chànggē
喝 茶　　看 书　　购物　　做 饭　　打 电玩　　唱歌

	朋友的名字	他/她喜欢……
1		
2		
3		
4		
5		

Congratulations!

Now that you have completed the practice activities for Unit 2, please complete the following self-assessment to see how much you know.

Listen to the recording and repeat the sentences you hear. Then read the responses and choose the correct reply for each question or statement. 🎧

1. A: 你今年多大了？
   B: _____

2. A: 你看起来真年轻。
   B: _____

3. A: 我喜欢喝茶。你呢？
   B: _____

4. A: 这是什么？
   B: _____

5. A: 这是李阿姨。
   B: _____

6. A: 今天我请客。
   B: _____

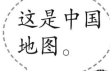
这是中国地图。

我今年20岁。

谢谢你！

李阿姨，您好！

我也喜欢喝茶。

你也很年轻。

你很棒！

Unit 3 Feel at Home Wherever You Are

Dì-sān dānyuán   Sì hǎi wéi jiā
第三单元   四 海 为 家

1 Listen to the recording and circle the correct syllables.

rì - lì	rén - lín	rè - lè	rèn - lùn
ràng - làng	xiǎo - qiǎo	nà - dà	gǒu - kǒu
sū - shū	jīng - yīng	bàn - pàn	tōng - dōng

2 Read the words aloud and circle the characters with neutral tone.

妈妈   爸爸   爷爷   奶奶   哥哥   姐姐

学生   医生   工作   留学生   有意思

3 Read the sentences aloud and mark the tones.

Ni jia you ji kou ren?
(1) A: 你家有几口人？

Wo jia you san kou ren.
B: 我家有三口人。

Ni shi na guo ren?
(2) A: 你是哪国人？

Wo shi Ribenren.
B: 我是日本人。

Ta qu bu qu xuexiao?
(3) A: 他去不去学校？

Ta bu qu xuexiao.   Ta qu gongsi.
B: 他不去学校。他去公司。

4 Listen carefully to the recording, then match the Chinese sentences with the correct Pinyin. Finally, match each question with the correct answer. 🎧

(1) 现在几点了?   Nǐ zuò shénme gōngzuò?

(2) 你是哪国人?   Xiànzài jǐ diǎn le?

(3) 你做什么工作?   Nǐ shì nǎ guó rén?

(4) 你家有几口人?   Nǐ jiā yǒu jǐ kǒu rén?

a. 我是美国人。   Xiànzài jiǔ diǎn.

b. 现在九点。   Wǒ shì Měiguórén.

c. 我是北京大学的留学生。   Wǒ shì Běijīng Dàxué de liúxuéshēng.

d. 我家有三口人。   Wǒ jiā yǒu sān kǒu rén.

Question: _____?

Answer: _____。

Question: _____?

Answer: _____。

Question: _____?

Answer: _____。

Question: _____?

Answer: _____。

5 Choose the proper labels for the characters in the pictures. One label may be used twice.

yéye yīshēng
爷爷 医生

| yéye 爷爷 | nǎinai 奶奶 | bàba 爸爸 | māma 妈妈 | jiějie 姐姐 | dìdi 弟弟 |

| yīshēng 医生 | lǎoshī 老师 | gōngsī jīnglǐ 公司 经理 | jiātíng zhǔfù 家庭主妇 | xuésheng 学生 |

6 Match each picture with the appropriate word.

爸爸　　妈妈　　爷爷　　奶奶　　弟弟　　姐姐

老师　　学生　　经理　　医生　　家庭主妇　　记者

7 Fill in the blanks with the given words.

> 在　　是　　现在　　和　　都

比尔＿＿＿珍妮的哥哥。他＿＿＿中国学汉语。他＿＿＿是北京大学的留学生。珍妮的爸爸是医生，妈妈＿＿＿老师，＿＿＿学校工作。比尔＿＿＿北京大学认识了山田。山田是日本人，大家＿＿＿叫他"小北京"。比尔＿＿＿山田都说汉语。他们都是中国通。

8 Create at least six phrases using 和.

| 先生 | 大爷 | 老师 | 女士 | 李丽 | 加拿大 |
| 大妈 | 英国 | 咖啡 | 比尔 | 学生 | 茶 |

(1) ＿＿＿＿＿＿＿＿＿＿＿　　(4) ＿＿＿＿＿＿＿＿＿＿＿

(2) ＿＿＿＿＿＿＿＿＿＿＿　　(5) ＿＿＿＿＿＿＿＿＿＿＿

(3) ＿＿＿＿＿＿＿＿＿＿＿　　(6) ＿＿＿＿＿＿＿＿＿＿＿

Grammar Practice

9 Write the time in Chinese.

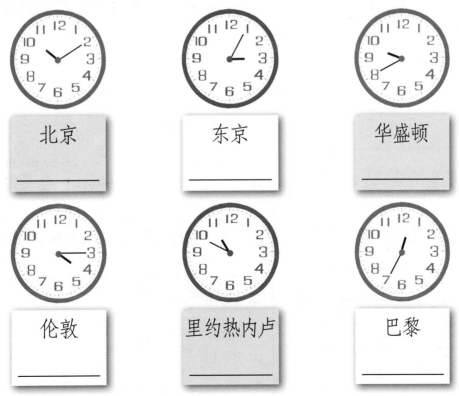

北京 ＿＿＿＿＿＿

东京 ＿＿＿＿＿＿

华盛顿 ＿＿＿＿＿＿

伦敦 ＿＿＿＿＿＿

里约热内卢 ＿＿＿＿＿＿

巴黎 ＿＿＿＿＿＿

10 Listen to the recording and repeat the sentences aloud. Then write down the missing parts. 🎧

(1) A: 你 <u>吃不吃</u> 比萨？   B: 我 **吃** 比萨。

(2) A: 他_____美国人？   B: 他 **是** 美国人。

(3) A: 你妈妈_____汉语？   B: 我妈妈不 **说** 汉语。

(4) A: 你_____打电玩？   B: 我很 **喜欢** 打电玩。

(5) A: 比尔_____个中国通？   B: 比尔 **是** 个中国通。

11 Change the 吗 questions into verb+不+verb questions. Then choose the correct responses from the box.

(1) 你喝咖啡吗？

A: 你喝不喝咖啡？

B: _____。

(2) 你们写汉字吗？

A: _____？

B: _____。

(3) 你认识比尔吗？

A: _____？

B: _____。

(4) 你哥哥是医生吗？

A: _____？

B: _____。

(5) 王老师是你的汉语老师吗？

A: _____？

B: _____。

Xièxie,   wǒ bù hē.
a. 谢谢，我 不 喝 。

Wǒ rènshi Bǐ'ěr,   tā shì wǒ de péngyou.
b. 我 认识 比尔，他 是 我 的 朋友 。

Wáng lǎoshī shì wǒ de Hànyǔ lǎoshī.
c. 王 老师 是 我 的 汉语 老师。

Wǒ gēge bú shì yīshēng.   Tā shì lǜshī.
d. 我 哥哥 不 是 医生 。他 是 律师。

Wǒmen xiě hànzì.
e. 我们 写 汉字。

12 Complete the questions with 哪. Then answer each question with your own information.

(1) A: 你是＿＿＿国人？

    B: ＿＿＿＿＿＿＿。

(2) A: 你喜欢＿＿＿个城市？

    B: ＿＿＿＿＿＿＿。

(3) A: 你是＿＿＿个大学的学生？

    B: ＿＿＿＿＿＿＿。

(4) A: 你希望在＿＿＿个公司工作？

    B: ＿＿＿＿＿＿＿。

13 Make questions using 哪.

(1) 她是中国人。   Question: ＿＿＿＿＿＿＿？

(2) 他在IBM公司工作。   Question: ＿＿＿＿＿＿＿？

(3) 李丽在北京大学学习。   Question: ＿＿＿＿＿＿＿？

(4) 比尔在中国留学。   Question: ＿＿＿＿＿＿＿？

Practical Training — Time Information

14 Find the time information in the pictures. Then choose the correct answers.

中国南方航空 CHINA SOUTHERN	登机牌 BOARDING PASS
航班 FLIGHT CZ3909	到达站 DESTN SHANGHAI	舱位等级 CLASS F	前舱座位 FRONT SEAT 3C
日期 DATE 05SEP09	登机口 GATE A02		后舱座位 REAR SEAT
姓名 NAME 王 军 WANG JUN		序号 No. 125
登机时间 BOARDING TIME 0930	ET 7646936598057／2

请勿折叠 DON'T FOLD
登机用于起飞前15分钟关闭 GATES CLOSE 15 MINUTES BEFORE DEPARTURE

大华国际影院 DAHUA INTERNATIONAL CINEMA	
时间 TIME	2011年12月20日 18:30开场
影片 MOVIE	金陵十三钗
座位 SEAT	15排20号
票价 PRICE	80.00元

(1) The flight most likely departs at:

    A. 上午九点一刻

    B. 上午十点

    C. 晚上九点半

(2) The film will begin at:

    A. 上午八点三十分

    B. 晚上六点三十分

    C. 早上六点三十分

第一学期课程表	
课 程\日 期\时间	星期一
上午 (9：00~12：00)	中国文化
下午 (14：30~16：30)	汉语
晚上 (18：30~21：00)	法语

新短信

下午三点见！

选项　　　　　退出

(3) The Chinese class begins at:

A. 上午九点

B. 下午两点三十分

C. 晚上六点三十分

(4) They will meet at:

A. 3：00

B. 15：00

C. 18：00

Writing Chinese Characters

15 **Write the sentences in Chinese, then read each one aloud.**

You want to ask an old lady what time it is. You would say:

_____

You want to know which country your classmate comes from. You would ask:

_____

You want to know how many family members your friend has. You would ask:

_____

You are not sure about whether your friend likes you or not. You would ask:

_____

16 **Practice writing the following Chinese characters.**

rì 丨冂日日

日

běi 丨⺊扌扌北

北

xué 丶丷丷丷兴学学学

学

xí 乛⺈习

习

shī 丨丿广广师师

师

yī 一丆丆丏丟医

医

jiā 丶丶宀宀宀宇宇家家家

家

gē 一丆丆丏可可哥哥哥哥

哥

xiàn 一丆丆王王丑玑现现

现

shuō 丶讠讠讦诮说说说

说

běn 一十才木本

本

jīng 丶亠亠卞亨京京

京

xiào 一十才木朾朾柠柠校校

校

lǎo 一十土耂老老

老

dà 一ナ大

大

shēng 丿⺊牛生生

生

bà 丶丷父父谷爸爸

爸

rén 丿人

人

zài 一ナ才在在在

在

zuò 丿亻亻仁仁佧佧做做做做

做

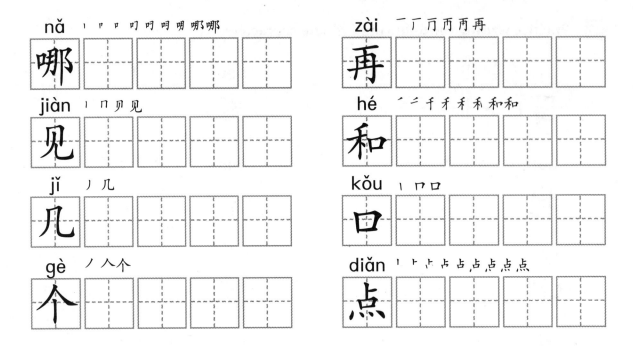

nǎ 丨 ⴖ 口 ⴖ ⴖ ⴖ 叩 哪 哪

哪

jiàn 丨 ⴖ 贝 见

见

jǐ 丿 几

几

gè 丿 人 个

个

zài 一 厂 万 币 再 再

再

hé 一 二 千 千 禾 禾 和 和

和

kǒu 丨 ⴖ 口

口

diǎn 丨 ⴖ ⴖ 占 占 占 点 点

点

Interpersonal Communication

17 Complete the conversations with the appropriate words.

(1) A: 托尼先生, 晚上好!

B: _____!

(2) A: ____, 您好!

B: _____!

(3) A: 王____, 再见!

B: _____!

18 Include a family photo and give a brief introduction of your family members.

我的全家福

我家有_____口人：_____、_____、_____、
_____、……和我。_____是_____，_____是_____，
_____是_____，_____是_____，……，我是_____。

19 Interview a classmate and record his or her answers.

Question: 你是哪国人？

Answer: _____。

Question: 你是哪个大学的学生？

Answer: _____。

Question: 你喜欢哪个城市？

Answer: _____。

Question: 你希望去哪个公司工作？

Answer: _____。

20 How do you address strangers in your first language? Compare with Chinese and describe your observations about the similarities and differences.

In _____ (your first language): _____

In Chinese: _____

My conclusion:

_____

_____

_____

Congratulations!

Now that you have completed the practice activities for Unit 3, please complete the following self-assessment to see how much you know.

The best time

Activities	The average student	You
qǐchuáng 起床	6:00	
chī zǎofàn 吃早饭	起床以后30分钟	
yùndòng 运动	8:00~9:00 16:00~17:00	
hē chá 喝茶	吃饭以后半个小时	
xuéxí 学习	9:00~11:00 14:00~16:00 19:00~21:00	
shuìjiào 睡觉	22:00	

你很棒!

Tip

qǐchuáng
起床　to get up

yǐhòu
以后　after

bàn gè xiǎoshí
半个小时
half an hour

Unit 4　In and Out of Class

Dì-sì dānyuán　Kè nèi kè wài

第四单元　课内课外

Pronunciation Practice

1 Read the words and circle the characters whose Pinyin begin with the initials *j, q, x*.

(学)校　最近　喜欢　姓名　高兴　今天　下课　去　家

见面　一起　酒吧　谢谢　不行　对不起　不客气

2 Read the words and circle the characters whose Pinyin begin with the initials *zh, ch, sh*.

多(少)　茶　听说　找　占座　上课　图书馆

周六　主演　大学生　宿舍　时候　知道

3 Read the following words aloud. Then classify the syllables according to their initials and finals.

zuìjìn 最近　jiànmiàn 见面　duìbuqǐ 对不起　yīqǐ 一起　shàngkè 上课　dāngrán 当然　yújiā 瑜伽

jìhuà 计划　yǐhòu 以后　pángtīng 旁听　diànyǐng 电影　Zhōuliù 周六　qù 去　chànggē 唱歌

Initial	
j	jiànmiàn _____
q	_____
zero initial	_____
	_____

Final	
ian	_____
ang	_____
ou	_____

4 Label each place in the picture with the appropriate word.

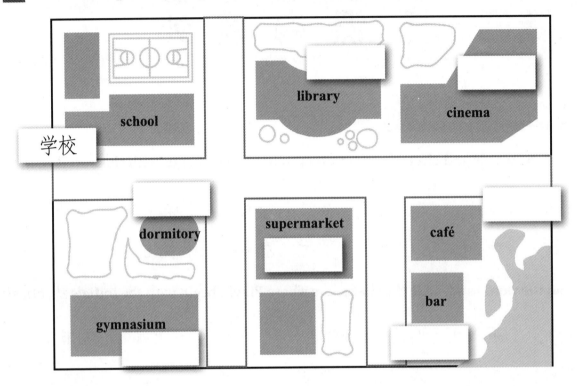

5 Choose and label each person with the appropriate word.

白领

经理

客户

大学生

父母

自由职业者

6 **Write down the words in proper boxes.**

túshūguǎn 图书馆　yǐhòu 以后　gōngsī 公司　xiàkè 下课　diàoyán 调研　zuìjìn 最近　diànyǐng 电影　diànyǐngyuàn 电影院

shàngkè 上课　shìchǎng 市场　zhàn zuò 占座　kāihuì 开会　chūchāi 出差　dǎgōng 打工　pángtīng 旁听　Zhōuliù 周六

About time:	About school life:	About work:

7 **Complete the conversations with the given words.**

kàn shū 看书　shàngwǎng 上网　dǎgōng 打工　chànggē 唱歌　tiàowǔ 跳舞　chīfàn 吃饭

(1) A: 你今天晚上做什么?

B: 我今天晚上去KTV_____。

(2) A: 你周末做什么?

B: 我周末去麦当劳_____。

(3) A: 你星期天做什么?

B: 我星期天和朋友一起去酒吧_____。

(4) A: 你下午做什么?

B: 我下午_____。

(5) A: 你中午十二点做什么?

B: 我中午十二点去_____。

(6) A: 你最近喜欢做什么?

B: 我最近喜欢去图书馆_____。

8 Match the people, places and activities, then create sentences with the related words.

公司经理	公司	出差
大学生	上海	工作
白领	家	上中国文化课
自由职业者	学校	开会

(1) _____

(2) _____

(3) _____

(4) _____

9 Choose a film and invite a friend to go to the movies together. Then fill in the blanks with the words in the box.

Wòhǔ-cánglóng
《 卧虎藏龙 》
Zhǔyǎn: Zhāng Zǐyí
主演：章 子怡

Xīn Jǐngchá Gùshi
《新 警察 故事》
Zhǔyǎn: Chéng Lóng
主演： 成 龙

Dù Lālā Shēngzhí Jì
《杜拉拉 升职 记》
Zhǔyǎn: Xú Jìnglěi
主演：徐 静蕾

什么	谁	一起	门口	他/她	不见不散	在

A: 你好！周六晚上＿＿＿＿去看电影好吗？

B: 最近有＿＿＿＿好电影？

A: 听说＿＿＿＿很好看。

B: ＿＿＿＿是主演？

A: 主演是＿＿＿＿。你喜欢＿＿＿＿吗？

B: 很喜欢。

A: 我们周六晚上七点_____电影院_____见，好吗？

B: 好的！_____！

A: 不见不散！

10 Complete the questions with 谁, 哪儿, 哪, 什么, 什么时候.

(1) A: 那是_____？

B: 那是我的汉语书。

(2) A: _____去麦当劳打工了？

B: 李小军去麦当劳打工了。

(3) A: 我们_____见面？

B: 今天下午两点见面，好吗？

(4) A: 我们在_____见面？

B: 在学校门口见面，好吗？

(5) A: _____部电影的主演是周润发？

B: 《孔子》的主演是周润发。

11 Create at least three sentences with the given words. How many sentences can you make?

| 比尔 | 山田 | KTV | 电影院 | 图书馆 | 咖啡厅 | 学校 |
| 上课 | 唱歌 | 咖啡 | 书 | 电影 | 去 | 看 | 喝 | 和 |

eg. 比尔去学校上课。

(1) _____

(2) _____

(3) _____

12 Complete the conversations with the given words. Then listen to the recording and repeat aloud.

> 哪　谁　哪儿　什么　听说　呢　吗　呀　吧

(1) A: 你去_____？
   B: 我去咖啡馆喝咖啡。
   A: 你和_____一起去？
   B: 我和珍妮一起去。

(2) A: 你周六做_____？
   B: 我周六去健身房打工。
   A: 你去_____个健身房打工？
   B: 我去学校门口的健身房打工。

(3) A: 你是成龙的粉丝_____？
   B: 对_____。你_____？
   A: 我也是。_____最近有成龙主演的电影，一起去看_____！
   B: 好主意!

Practical Training — Making Plans

13 Create a schedule for your weekend.

周六:

_____

_____

_____

周日:

_____

_____

_____

Choose activities from this list or come up with activities of your own.

去学校学习

去公司工作

去电影院看电影

去健身房健身

去图书馆看书

去咖啡馆见朋友

14 **Write the sentences in Chinese, then read each one aloud.**

You want to invite your friend to go to the movies together this weekend. You would say:

_____

You intend to decline an invitation. You would say:

_____

You want to know whether your friend has free time or not. You would ask:

_____

You want to say you will wait for him/her until he/she comes. You would say:

_____

15 **Read the following characters. Then try to figure out what they have in common.**

听　咖　啡　吧　呀　吗　哪　唱　喝

All of these characters _____

16 **Practice writing the following Chinese characters.**

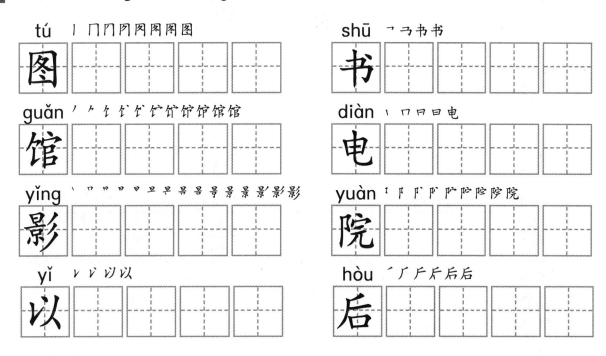

tú　丨 冂 冂 门 冈 冈 图 图　图

shū　乛 书 书 书　书

guǎn　丿 夕 夕 夕 夕 炉 炉 馆 馆 馆 馆　馆

diàn　丨 冂 曰 日 电　电

yǐng　丨 冂 冂 日 旦 旦 昰 昰 景 景 景 影 影 影　影

yuàn　阝 阝 阝 阝 阾 阾 陊 院 院　院

yǐ　丶 丷 以 以　以

hòu　丿 厂 厂 后 后 后　后

zhōu) 刀月月冎用周周

周

jìn ´ 厂 斤 斤 斤 近近

近

yǎn `丶氵氵沪沪沪沪滈演演演

演

huà ノイイ化

化

xià 一丁下

下

páng `亠亠岭产产产宇宇旁

旁

zhàn l 卜卜占占

占

jiàn l 冂冂见见

见

duì フ又 又 对对

对

me ノ么么

么

zǒu 一十十卡卡走走

走

zhǎo 一十十才找找找

找

zuì `丨冂日旦旦早早昂昻最最

最

zhǔ `一二主主

主

wén `一ナ文

文

shàng l 卜上

上

kè `讠讠讱讱讱课课

课

tīng l 冂口叮听听听

听

zuò `亠广广庐庐庐座座

座

miàn 一一厂厂面面面面面

面

zěn ノ广午午午乍乍怎怎怎

怎

yàng 一十才木术术栏栏样样

样

chàng `丨冂口叩叩唱唱唱唱

唱

17 Complete the conversations with the correct responses from the box.

> a. 对不起，我有约了。
>
> b. 好啊。我们去哪儿唱歌？
>
> c. 对不起，我最近没有空儿。
>
> d. 干吗这么客气？

(1) A: 周末一起去KTV唱歌好吗？

    B: _____

(2) A: 可以请你喝杯咖啡吗？

    B: _____

(3) A: 谢谢你。今天我请你吃饭。

    B: _____

(4) A: 你最近有空儿吗？

    B: _____

18 Listen to the recording and repeat the sentences. Then choose the appropriate responses from the box.

(1) A: 周末我们去老街拍照，怎么样？

    B: _____

(2) A: 今晚八点在咖啡厅见面，怎么样？

    B: _____

(3) A: 我去旁听你们的中国文化课，怎么样？

    B: _____

> a. 对不起，今晚不行，我没空儿。
>
> b. 没问题！
>
> c. 好主意！
>
> d. 很棒！
>
> e. 不怎么样。
>
> f. 他是个中国通。

(4) A: 比尔的汉语怎么样?

　　B: _____

(5) A: 李芳的瑜伽老师怎么样?

　　B: _____

(6) A: 那部电影怎么样?

　　B: _____

Tip

Bù zěnmeyàng
不　怎么样

means "not very
well". It expresses an
unsatisfactory opinion
about something.

19 Interview three friends to discover what they like to do in their leisure time, then record their answers in Chinese.

	姓名	国籍 (nationality)	喜欢……
e.g.	山田	日本	喜欢去学校旁听文化课
1			
2			
3			

20 Invite some friends to join you for tea, recording their answers. Take special notes of any refusals to your invitation, then draw a conclusion about how many people refused your invitation and try to explain the reasons.

Question: 一起去上汉语课,怎么样?

Answers:

　　(1) _____
　　(2) _____
　　(3) _____
　　(4) _____
　　(5) _____

My conclusion:

_____

_____

_____

Now that you have completed the practice activities for Unit 4, please complete the following self-assessment to see how much you know.

Fill in as much of the schedule as you can in Chinese.

我的一周计划

	上午	下午	晚上
星期一			
星期二			
星期三			
星期四			
星期五			
星期六			
星期日			

你很棒！

Unit 5

Shopping and Bargaining

Dì-wǔ dānyuán   Tǎo jià huán jià
第五单元   讨 价 还 价

1 Listen to the recording and circle the correct syllables.

(mǎi) – mài	zuì – huì	xiǎng – xiǎn	lù – lù
lán – nán	qián – qiǎn	tiáo – táo	zāi – zhāi
liàng – làng	xù – sù	shuāng – shāng	wǎng – wǎn

2 Write the Pinyin for each word and mark the actual tones of 一.

yíyàng					
一样	一个	一件	一起	一本	一块

一杯	一条	一辆	一点儿	一元

3 Write the Pinyin for each word and mark the actual tones of the 3rd tone.

xǐhuan					
喜欢	砍价	好看	怎么样	哪里	请客

美国	老师	以后	老板	粉色	美元

4 **Listen to the recording, then match the Chinese sentences with the correct Pinyin. Finally, match each question with the correct answer.** 🎧

(1) 为什么我的裤子比你的贵？　　Néng yòng xìnyòngkǎ ma?

(2) 能用信用卡吗？　　Wèishénme wǒ de kùzi bǐ nǐ de guì?

(3) 你喜欢哪个颜色？　　Nǐmen yǒu hēisè de zìxíngchē ma?

(4) 你们有黑色的自行车吗？　　Nǐ xǐhuan nǎge yánsè?

a. 我喜欢蓝色和粉色。　　Wǒmen zhǐ yǒu hóngsè hé lǜsè de.

b. 我们只有红色和绿色的。　　Yīnwèi wǒ bǐ nǐ huì kǎnjià.

c. 因为我比你会砍价。　　Duìbuqǐ, wǒmen zhǐ shōu xiànjīn.

d. 对不起，我们只收现金。　　Wǒ xǐhuan lánsè hé fěnsè.

Question: _____?　　Question: _____?

Answer: _____。　　Answer: _____。

Question: _____?　　Question: _____?

Answer: _____。　　Answer: _____。

Vocabulary Practice

5 **Match each picture with the appropriate word.**

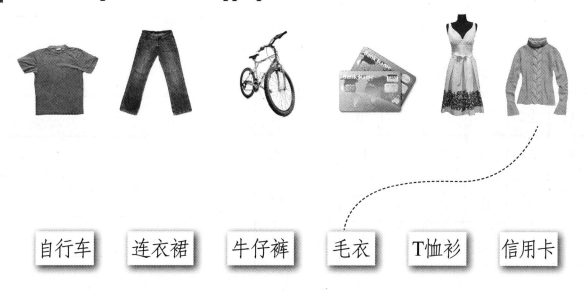

自行车　　连衣裙　　牛仔裤　　毛衣　　T恤衫　　信用卡

6 Match each object to the appropriate measure word.

件　辆
条　双

7 Can you identify all the words in the puzzle? Pick them out and write the characters and their meanings on the lines.

三	黑	一	起	合	稍	衣	商
牛	因	为	连	样	砍	价	适
仔	共	什	衣	服	蓝	格	自
裤	子	么	裙	最	老	师	行
站	低	外	白	低	板	车	现
板	随	便	套	价	钱	金	不
衫	场	宜	白	天	购	红	错
网	购	颜	色	物	黄	卡	粉

一起together _____ _____

_____ _____

_____ _____

_____ _____

_____ _____

_____ _____

_____ _____

_____ _____

8 **Answer the questions according to the information given.**

¥ 320元
蓝色

¥ 260元
白色

(1) 外套比毛衣_____。(A. 贵 / B. 便宜)

(2) 毛衣的颜色比外套的颜色_____。(A. 浅 / B. 深)

¥ 280元
黄色

¥ 350元
粉色

(3) 两件连衣裙_____。(A. 一样 / B. 不一样)

(4) 两件衣服，_____更便宜。(A. 黄色的 / B. 粉色的)

9 **Color the clothes with your favorite colors, then describe them with proper words.**

Recommended colors:

| 白色 | 蓝色 | 黑色 | 粉色 | 绿色 | 黄色 | 红色 |

他穿着一件（　　　）的外套、一件（　　　）的衬衫、一条（　　　）的牛仔裤和一双（　　　）的运动鞋。她穿着一件（　　　）的连衣裙和一双（　　　）的皮鞋。

Grammar Practice

10 Fill in the blanks with correct measure words.

| 双 | 件 | 条 | 辆 | 杯 | 个 | 块 |

(1) 三_____蛋糕　　(4) 一_____外套　　(7) 两_____牛仔裤

(2) 这_____鞋　　(5) 一_____可乐　　(8) 一_____自行车

(3) 十_____钱　　(6) 五_____人

11 Change 比/不比 into 没有.

(1) 比尔比李丽高。

_____

(2) 外套不比T恤衫便宜。

_____

(3) 粉色的自行车比黄色的自行车漂亮。

_____

(4) 我不比你年轻。

_____

12 **Complete the conversations with 只 and 了.**

(1) A: 你买衣服花_____多少钱？

   B: 我_____花_____150元。

(2) A: 比尔，你去商场买_____什么东西？

   B: 我_____买_____一双鞋。

(3) A: 可以再便宜一点儿吗？

   B: 不行，这是最低价_____。

(4) A: 李丽，你昨天去哪儿_____？

   B: 我昨天去看_____一场电影。

13 **Fill in the blanks with the given words.**

> 件　太　怎么样　多少　便宜　了　不　块

A: 这_____衣服_____钱？

B: 260_____钱。

A: _____贵_____！能不能_____点儿？

B: 这是最低价。

A: 我_____买了。

B: 好吧，好吧，230元卖给你。

A: 200元_____？

B: 真的不行。

14 Imagine you are the manager of an online clothing store. Add prices and information about each garment for your website.

T恤衫	毛衣	连衣裙	外套
¥: __90元__	¥: _____	¥: _____	¥: _____
颜色: __红、蓝、__	颜色: _____	颜色: _____	颜色: _____
__白__	_____	_____	_____

牛仔裤	皮鞋	围巾
¥: _____	¥: _____	¥: _____
颜色: _____	颜色: _____	颜色: _____
_____	_____	_____

How would you like to advertise your products?

_____

_____

Tip

wùměi-jiàlián
物美价廉
high quality and inexpensive

15 Write the price in Chinese.

¥: 360元

_____

¥: 80元

_____

¥: 24元

_____

¥: 30元

_____

¥: 119元

_____

¥: 128元

_____

¥: 2800元

_____

16 Write the sentences in Chinese, then read each one aloud.

You want to know how much your friend's shoes cost. You would say:

_____

Your friend isn't taller than you or he/she is the same height as you. You would say:

_____

Your friend's coat is exactly like Bill's. You would say:

_____

You want to exchange your shirt with a blue one. You would say:

_____

17 **Practice writing the following Chinese characters.**

yán `、一ソァ立产产彦彦彦彦颜颜颜颜`
颜

sè `′ク夕名多色`
色

hóng `ㄥ纟纟纟红红`
红

fěn `、ソ斗半米米粉粉粉`
粉

hēi `丶口四四日甲甲里里黑黑黑`
黑

qián `ノノ广上丰钅钅钅钱钱钱`
钱

měi `、ソ丷艹半羊兰美美`
美

yuán `一二テ元`
元

yī `、一亡ナ衣衣`
衣

fú `刀月月月肌肌服服`
服

zì `′ノ自自自自`
自

xíng `ノク彳彳行行`
行

chē `一七左车`
车

lǎo `一十土严老老`
老

bǎn `一十才木木杉杤板`
板

huā `一十艹艹扩花花`
花

mǎi `フ乛罒乛买买`
买

mài `一十士去卉壶卖卖`
卖

kǎn `一ノ丆丆石矶矶砍`
砍

jià `ノイ亻伈价价`
价

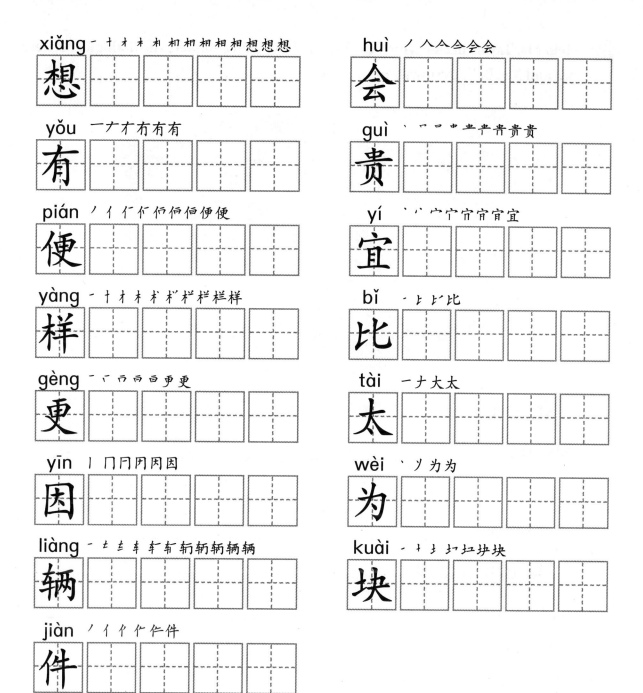

18 Help Ms. Taylor decide which clothing to buy, then complete the dialogue between her and Ms. Bell, the owner of the shop.

Ms. Bell：你好！要买点儿什么？

Ms. Taylor：_____。

Ms. Bell：你看_____怎么样？

Ms. Taylor：_____。

Ms. Bell：180块。

Ms. Taylor：_____？

Ms. Bell：不行。

Ms. Taylor：_____。

Ms. Bell：这样吧，150块，最低价，怎么样？

Ms. Taylor：_____。

19 **Interview five friends to find out how tall they are, then record and compare them.**

	姓名	身高（height）
1		
2		
3		
4		
5		

My conclusion:

_____比_____高。_____比_____更高。

_____最高。_____和 _____没有_____高。

_____和 _____一样高。

20 **Interview your family members to find out their favorite colors. Record as much information as possible in Chinese.**

爸爸最喜欢的颜色是_____，因为_____。

妈妈最喜欢的颜色是_____，因为_____。

_____最喜欢的颜色是_____，因为_____。

_____最喜欢的颜色是_____，因为_____。

_____最喜欢的颜色是_____，因为_____。

_____最喜欢的颜色是_____，因为_____。

Now that you have completed the practice activities for Unit 5, please complete the following self-assessment to see how much you know.

Listen and record, then write the correct answers in the table. 🎧

衣服	颜色	价格	和朋友的一样/不一样
牛仔裤			
连衣裙			
外套			
毛衣			
T恤衫			
鞋			

你很棒！

Unit 6　Fine Food

Dì-liù dānyuán　Tiān xià měi shí
第六单元　天下美食

Pronunciation Practice

1 Listen carefully to the recording and read the words. Then circle the characters whose Pinyin end with –n.

（粉）色　　　因为　　　自行车　　　米饭　　　白糖　　　学问

免费　　　一边　　　为什么　　　文化　　　电话　　　饭馆

2 Read the following words aloud. Then circle the syllables with the 3rd tone.

（mǐfàn）米饭　　yǐnliào 饮料　　fànguǎnr 饭馆儿　　mǎidān 买单　　shuǐguǒ 水果　　shuǐ 水　　diǎncài 点菜　　zhǔshí 主食

huǒguō 火锅　　hǎochī 好吃　　děng 等　　miǎnfèi 免费　　dāngrán 当然　　jiǎozi 饺子　　guǒzhī 果汁　　Běijīng kǎoyā 北京烤鸭

3 Listen to the recording and read the words aloud.

这儿　　　那儿　　　哪儿　　　一点儿　　　吃点儿

喝点儿　　买点儿　　等座儿　　菜名儿　　一边儿

4 Listen to the recording and repeat the sentences after you hear them.

Wǒ è le, jīntiān xiǎng chī diǎnr là de.
我饿了，今天想吃点儿辣的。

Wǒmen kěyǐ yìbiān děng zuò, yìbiān chī miǎnfèi shuǐguǒ.
我们可以一边等座，一边吃免费水果。

Zhège cài jiào shénme míngzi? Wǒ cónglái méi chīguo.

这个 菜 叫 什么 名字？ 我 从来 没 吃过。

Zhōngguó càimíng zhēn yǒu xuéwen a!

中国 菜名 真 有 学问 啊！

Nàr de huǒguō wèidào tèbié hǎo.

那儿 的 火锅 味道 特别 好。

Vocabulary Practice

5 **Match each word with the appropriate picture.**

水　　汤　　米饭　　面条　　饺子　　果汁

白糖　　火锅　　水果　　饮料　　西红柿　　北京烤鸭

6 Label each dish with the appropriate name.

_____ _____ _____

_____ _____ _____

Zhájiàngmiàn   Tángcùyú   Gōngbǎo Jīdīng   Shuǐzhǔyú   Mápó Dòufu   Suānlàtāng
a. 炸酱面 b. 糖醋鱼 c. 宫保 鸡丁 d. 水煮鱼 e. 麻婆豆腐 f. 酸辣汤

7 Match each food with its taste.

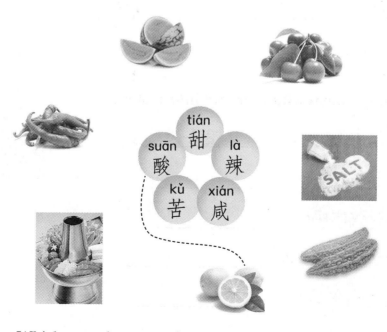

tián 甜
suān 酸
là 辣
kǔ 苦
xián 咸

Which taste do you prefer? _____

8 Write a description of a restaurant you know well, using as many of the given words as possible. Then share your description with your classmates.

饭馆　　菜　　　饮料　　水果　　味道　　服务　　座　　美元

钱　　　周到　　贵　　　好吃　　特别　　便宜　　辣　　甜

因为　　请客　　吃　　　喝　　　点 (v.)

Grammar Practice

9 Complete the dialogues with the given words.

zěnmeyàng	guo	nǎge	hǎochī	là	là de	kěyǐ
怎么样	过	哪个	好吃	辣	辣的	可以

A: 你吃＿＿＿＿中国菜吗？

B: 吃＿＿＿＿。

A: 中国菜的味道＿＿＿＿？

B: 很＿＿＿＿！

A: 你喜欢吃＿＿＿＿中国菜？

B: 我喜欢吃重庆辣子鸡。

A: 这个菜很＿＿＿＿, 你＿＿＿＿吃吗？

B: 可以。我喜欢吃＿＿＿＿。

> **Tip**
>
> Chóngqìng Làzijī
> 重庆　辣子鸡
> is a typical Sichuan dish in China.

10 Answer the questions with your own information.

(1) 你去过中国吗？　　　_没去过_____。

(2) 你吃过饺子吗？　　　＿＿＿＿＿＿＿＿＿。

(3) 你写过汉字吗？　　　＿＿＿＿＿＿＿＿＿。

(4) 你上过汉语课吗？　　＿＿＿＿＿＿＿＿＿。

(5) 你见过比尔吗？　　　＿＿＿＿＿＿＿＿＿。

(6) 你喝过中国茶吗？　　＿＿＿＿＿＿＿＿＿。

11 Give choices to Jenny using "是……还是……".

(1) 你是吃米饭还是吃面条？

 吃米饭。

(2) _____？

 喝水。

(3) _____？

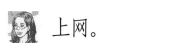 去跳舞。

(4) _____？

 上网。

(5) _____？

去超市。

12 Match each sentence with the appropriate picture.

(1) 爷爷一边看书一边喝茶。

(2) 我们一边唱歌一边跳舞。

(3) 妹妹一边吃菜一边喝果汁。

(4) 安娜一边上网一边学习。

13 **Fill in the blanks according to Episodes 1 and 2 in the Student Book.**

(1) 今天比尔想吃点儿辣_____。

(2) 比尔_____李丽去"海底捞"吃火锅。

(3) 他们_____等座，_____吃免费水果。

(4) 珍妮_____吃_____"火山飞雪"。

(5) 中国菜名_____有学问。

(6) 那儿的火锅味道_____好。

Practical Training — Chinese Dishes

14 **Order dishes for Bill and Li Li according to their preferences.**

 我喜欢吃辣的。   我喜欢吃甜的。

给比尔点菜：   给李丽点菜：

_____   _____

① Huǒshān Fēixuě
火山　飞雪

② Làzijī
辣子鸡

③ Tángcùyú
糖醋鱼

④ Suānlàtāng
酸辣汤

⑤ Tángcù Lǐji
糖醋里脊

⑥ Sìchuān Huǒguō
四川　火锅

15 **Do you know how to make the Chinese dish** 火山飞雪? **Please find the information through the Internet, try to complete the recipe below, and practice it at home if possible.**

菜名: 火山飞雪

味道: ＿＿＿＿＿＿＿、＿＿＿＿＿＿

食材 (ingredients) : ＿＿＿＿＿＿＿、＿＿＿＿＿＿

做法 (how to make it) :

(1) ＿＿＿＿＿＿＿＿＿＿＿＿＿＿＿＿＿＿＿＿

(2) ＿＿＿＿＿＿＿＿＿＿＿＿＿＿＿＿＿＿＿＿

(3) ＿＿＿＿＿＿＿＿＿＿＿＿＿＿＿＿＿＿＿＿

Writing Chinese Characters

16 **Write the sentences in Chinese, then read each one aloud.**

You want to invite your friend to have a dinner this weekend. You would say:

＿＿＿＿＿＿＿＿＿＿＿＿＿＿＿＿＿＿＿＿＿＿＿＿＿＿

You intend to order some Chinese dishes in a Chinese restaurant. You would say:

＿＿＿＿＿＿＿＿＿＿＿＿＿＿＿＿＿＿＿＿＿＿＿＿＿＿

You want to know whether Jenny wants to eat rice or noodles. You would ask:

＿＿＿＿＿＿＿＿＿＿＿＿＿＿＿＿＿＿＿＿＿＿＿＿＿＿

You want to describe a person who is dancing and singing. You would say:

＿＿＿＿＿＿＿＿＿＿＿＿＿＿＿＿＿＿＿＿＿＿＿＿＿＿

17 Practice writing the following Chinese characters.

miàn 一 丆 丆 丙 而 而 而 面 面
面

tiáo ノ 夂 夂 冬 条 条 条
条

mǐ 丶 丷 一 半 米 米
米

fàn ノ 勹 勹 饣 饣 饣 饭 饭
饭

shuǐ 刂 才 水 水
水

guǒ 丶 冂 冂 田 旦 甲 果 果
果

yǐn ノ 勹 勹 饣 饣 饣 饮 饮
饮

liào 丶 冫 一 半 米 米 米 米 料 料
料

huǒ 丶 丷 火 火
火

guō ノ 勹 勹 钅 钅 钅 钊 钊 钖 钖 锅 锅
锅

guǎn ノ 勹 勹 饣 饣 饣 饣 馆 馆 馆 馆
馆

wèi 丶 冂 口 口 吽 吽 味 味
味

dào 丶 丷 一 一 产 芦 芦 首 首 道 道
道

děng ノ 勹 勹 勹 竺 竺 竺 竺 笁 笁 等 等
等

zuò 丶 冫 广 广 广 庐 庐 庐 座 座
座

diǎn 丨 冖 占 占 占 点 点 点 点
点

cài 一 艹 艹 艹 艹 芯 芯 苹 苹 菜 菜
菜

wèn 丶 冂 门 门 问 问 问
问

fú ノ 月 月 月 月 肝 肝 服 服
服

wù ノ 勹 夂 冬 务 务
务

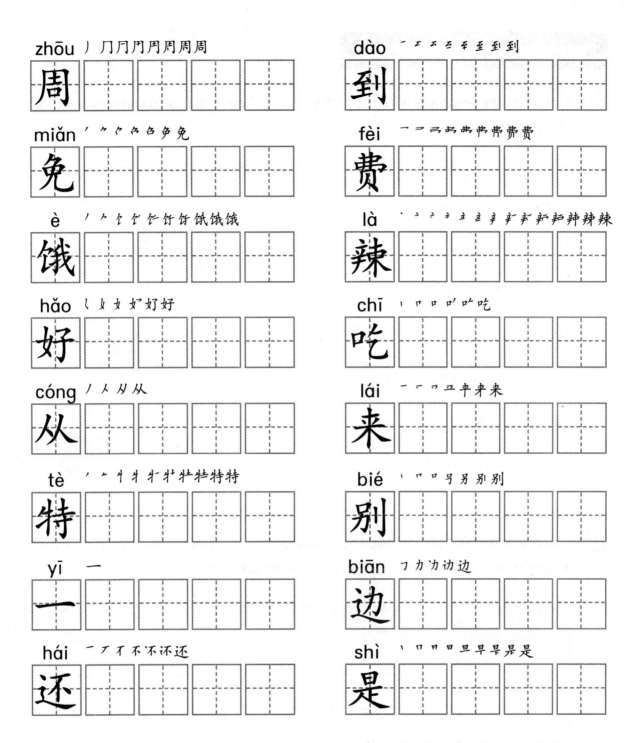

zhōu 丿 刀 刀 肎 肎 用 周 周

周

dào 一 工 工 互 至 至 到 到

到

miǎn 丿 夕 夕 夕 台 免 免

免

fèi 一 二 弓 弗 弗 帯 帯 费 费

费

è 丿 勺 勺 钅 钅 饣 饣 伩 饿 饿

饿

là 一 亠 ⺶ 亖 主 束 束 束 束 辨 辣 辣

辣

hǎo 乚 ⼥ ⼥ ⼥ 好 好

好

chī 丨 冂 口 口⺊ 吖 吃

吃

cóng 丿 人 从 从

从

lái 一 一 ㄣ 立 平 来 来

来

tè 丿 ⺧ 牜 牛 牛 牜 牜 牜 特 特 特

特

bié 丨 口 口 吕 另 别 别

别

yī 一

一

biān フ カ ⼒ 边 边 边

边

hái 一 厂 才 不 不 还 还

还

shì 丨 口 日 日 旦 早 早 是 是

是

18 Complete the sentences with the given words. Then match each conversation with the correct picture.

吃这个　　请坐　　请客

(1) A: 您_____!

B: 你坐, 你坐!

(2) A: 您_____! 这个菜最好吃!

B: 谢谢, 你也吃啊。

(3) A: 今天我_____!

B: 我请, 我请!

19 Interview five friends, asking them about their favorite Chinese dishes and what kinds of tastes they prefer. Then record their answers.

	姓名	国籍 (nationality)	最喜欢的中国菜	最喜欢的口味
e.g.	Susan	美国	糖醋里脊	甜
1				
2				
3				
4				
5				

20 Search for at least three Chinese dishes on the Internet. Figure out the taste of each dish, then recommend them to your family members or friends according to their preferences.

	菜名	味道	推荐给谁
e.g.	四川火锅	辣	
1			
2			
3			

家 常 菜

精美热菜		精美凉菜	
Làzijī 辣子鸡	25元	Chóngqìng Kǒushuǐjī 重庆 口水鸡	15元
Tángcù Lǐji 糖醋里脊	20元	Shíshū Lāpí 时蔬拉皮	10元
Yúxiāng Ròusī 鱼香肉丝	12元	Bōcài Huāshēngmǐ 菠菜花生米	8元
Mùxūròu 木须肉	12元	Liángbàn Jīnzhēngū 凉拌 金针菇	8元
Jiācháng Dòufu 家常 豆腐	12元	Pídàn Dòufu 皮蛋豆腐	6元
Dìsānxiān 地三鲜	10元	Sìchuān Pàocài 四川 泡菜	5元
Gōngbǎo Jīdīng 宫保 鸡丁	12元	Shuǐguǒ Shālā 水果 沙拉	12元
Tǔdòu Shāo Niúròu 土豆烧牛肉	20元	Pāi Huángguā 拍 黄瓜	6元
Jīngjiàng Ròusī 京酱 肉丝	18元	Liángbàn Hǎidàisī 凉拌 海带丝	6元
Sōngrén Yùmǐ 松仁 玉米	16元	Liángbàn Hēimù'ěr 凉拌 黑木耳	8元

Congratulations!

Now that you have completed the practice activities for Unit 6, please complete the following self-assessment to see how much you know.

Imagine that you are ordering something in a Chinese restaurant. Choose the correct responses in the box and complete the conversation below.

a. 可以啊！

b. 您是说西红柿拌白糖吗？

c. 我要饺子。

d. 是的。我特别喜欢吃甜的。

e. 我想吃甜的中国菜。

f. 对。给我来一份儿。

g. 你们有什么主食？

服务员：您想吃点儿什么？

顾　客：＿＿＿＿＿＿＿＿＿＿＿＿＿＿

服务员：来份儿糖醋里脊可以吗？

顾　客：＿＿＿＿＿＿＿＿＿＿＿＿＿＿

服务员：好的。

顾　客：你们这儿有"火山飞雪"吗？

服务员：＿＿＿＿＿＿＿＿＿＿＿＿＿＿

顾　客：＿＿＿＿＿＿＿＿＿＿＿＿＿＿

服务员：好的，一份糖醋里脊，一份火山飞雪。看起来您真喜欢吃甜的。

顾　客：＿＿＿＿＿＿＿＿＿＿＿＿＿＿

服务员：您点什么主食？

顾　客：＿＿＿＿＿＿＿＿＿＿＿＿＿＿

服务员：有面条、米饭、饺子。

顾　客：＿＿＿＿＿＿＿＿＿＿＿＿＿＿

你很棒！

Tip

When ordering dishes in a Chinese restaurant, some common expressions are:

Lái fènr ...
来份儿……
e.g. 来份儿宫保鸡丁

Wǒ yào ...
我 要……
e.g. 我要一瓶果汁。